Find Santa Claus

as He Brings Christmas Joy

Illustrated by Jerry Tiritilli

Louis Weber, C.E.O.
Publications International, Ltd.
7373 North Cicero Avenue
Lincolnwood, Illinois 60646

Manufactured in the U.S.A.

8 7 6 5 4 3

ISBN 1-56173-161-7

PUBLICATIONS INTERNATIONAL, LTD.

GO ROCKETS!

Everyone loves to decorate for Christmas! And of course, "yours truly" appears in many wonderful decorations. Check out this craft show—I'm a hot item this year! See if you can find me in all these crafts. Don't forget to find the real me, too!

2 Santa cookies

A Santa stocking

A wooden Santa doll

A Santa wreath

A Santa lamp

A Santa quilt

A Santa pillow

Santa in a centerpiece

REST ROOM ←

GO TEAM!

ROCKETS

BUY RAFFL HER $1⁰⁰ EACH OR 6 F WIN A DOOR

FRUIT CAKE $$ $$ WE'LL PAY YOU

How do I know not to bring you the same toys your parents are giving you? I visit toy stores and watch what people buy! Toy stores are almost as busy as my workshop at the North Pole—kids are always getting lost there. First, try to find me. Then see if you can find these lost children.

Bobby the Kid

Mini-Muscles, the Wonder Baby

Drummond Bugle, III

I. Wright Ticketts

Lil' Topknot

Mona Lisa Murphy

Chuckles and Giggles, the twin clowns

Presto Change-o

Hi Long Leggs, Jr.

One of my favorite things about Christmas is that I get to visit with girls and boys who come to see me at shopping malls. Shopping malls can be pretty crazy at Christmas, though! I'm taking a break right now. Can you find me? Can you find these crazy Christmas shoppers, too?

Tarzan

Candi Cotton

Moe Hawk

Kringles the Klown

Curly Wiggs

Leif Eric's son

Mother Goose

M. T. Pocketts

Christmas is only a few days away. And if you think it is busy at your house, you should see my workshop! Do you think I'll be ready for my Christmas Eve ride? After you find me, help me find these toys to fill my sack. We'd better check the list twice!

A red wagon

A train

A doll

A tricycle

A teddy bear

A ball

A skateboard

A truck

'Twas the night before Christmas,
    and all through these houses,
People were still up,
    Including some mouses!
Well, this isn't *exactly* the way my
favorite poem goes, but my way is
more realistic! See if you can find me,
and then see if you can spot these
Christmas Eve classics.

Cookies and milk
left out for me

A mouse not
stirring

This stocking
hung by the
chimney with care

2 fathers in
sleeping caps

Sugarplums
dancing

4 children nestled
all snug in
their beds

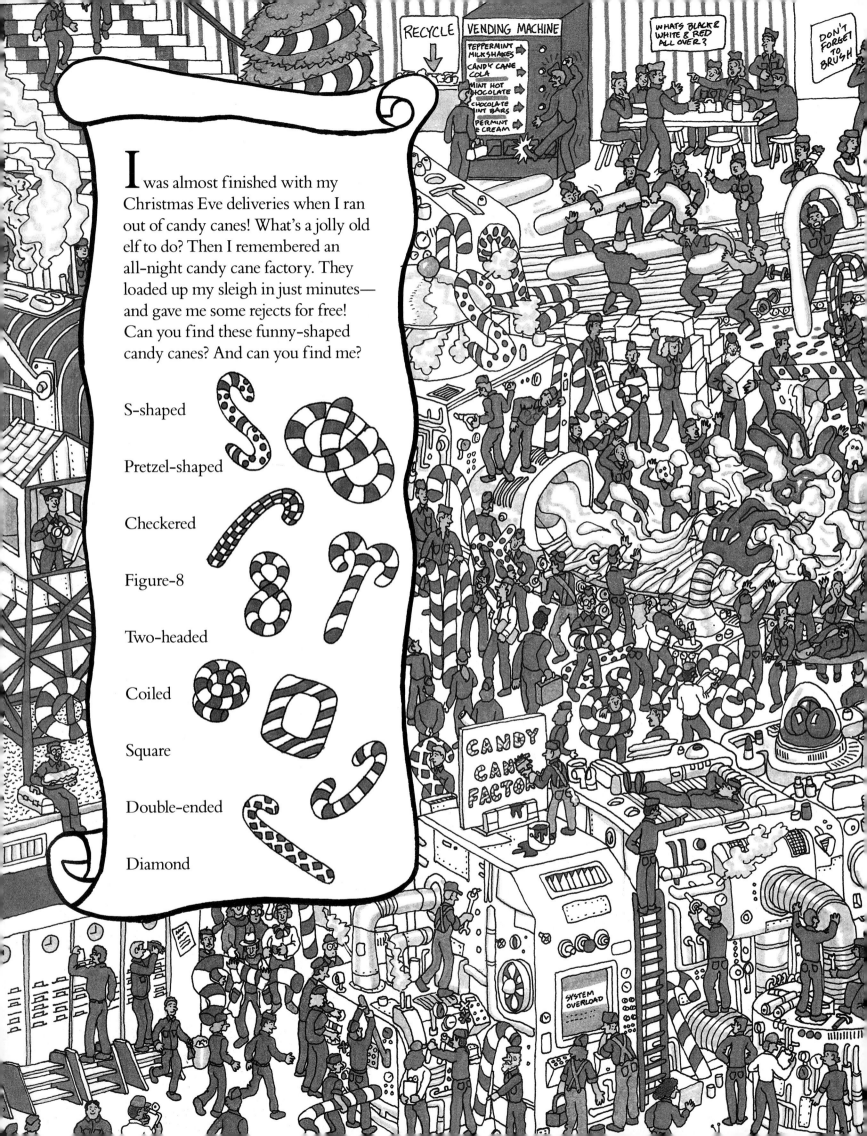

I was almost finished with my Christmas Eve deliveries when I ran out of candy canes! What's a jolly old elf to do? Then I remembered an all-night candy cane factory. They loaded up my sleigh in just minutes—and gave me some rejects for free! Can you find these funny-shaped candy canes? And can you find me?

S-shaped

Pretzel-shaped

Checkered

Figure-8

Two-headed

Coiled

Square

Double-ended

Diamond

Most people think I only fly through the air to deliver Christmas gifts. The mermaids, mermen, and other sea creatures will tell you differently. In fact, I swim so well, they think I'm one of them! Can you find me? Can you find this other silly sea stuff?

A Christmas seal

All eight of my reindeer

An angelfish

A catfish

5 notes in bottles

A peanut-butter-and-jellyfish

A submarine

A hammerhead shark

I had "wrapped up" my Christmas Eve rounds, when I realized I hadn't wrapped my gift to Mrs. Claus yet! I stopped off at Worldwide Gift Wrap, Inc. to see if they could help me out. Boy, were they busy! I decided to wrap Mrs. Claus's fuzzy slippers myself. After you find me, see if you can find these things that will help me wrap my gift.

A pair of yellow scissors

A red ruler

A stapler

Candy-cane wrapping paper

A pencil

A green tape dispenser

A snowman card

A green shoebox

CARDS & TAGS DEPARTMENT

RIBBONS & BOWS DEPARTMENT

WORLDWIDE GIFT WRAP, INC.
We've got it covered!

GIFT WRAP WHILE-U-WAIT

SNACK BAR

BOSS' OFFICE

BOX DEPARTMENT

PAPER PRINTING PRESSES

Mrs. Santa thinks I've put on a little weight lately. She suggested I take up skiing and skating. The ski lessons were fun, but it went downhill after that! After you find me, see if you can find these other silly skiers and skaters.

A real rockin' skier

A skier in a fur coat

A real cool dude

Somebody who's all "wrapped up" in skiing

"Duck!"

A skier who's "out of this world!"

A "figure" skater

Wroger Wrongway

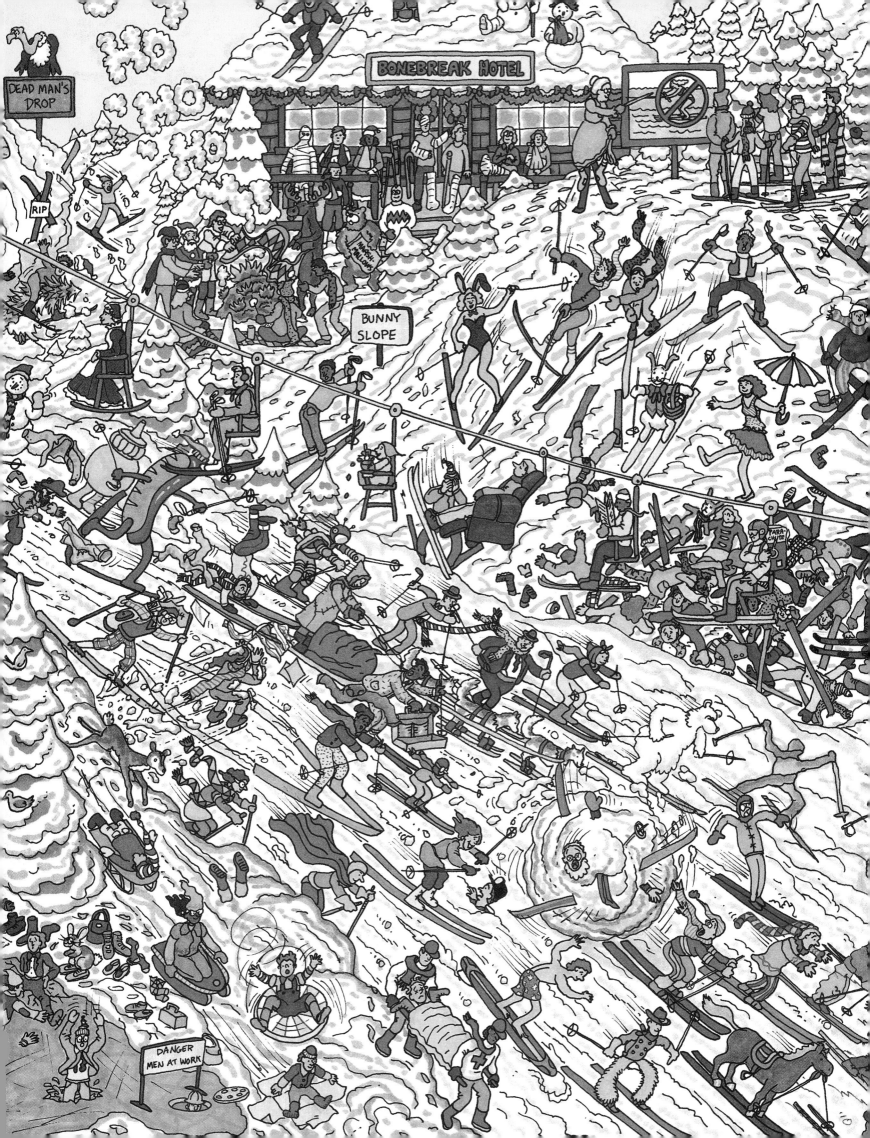

Take another look at the houses in *The Night Before Christmas* scene. Can you find these other funny things?

☐ Grandma got run over by a reindeer
☐ A Frantic Dad
☐ A Sudsy "Santa"
☐ A "cool" dog house
☐ A cat burglar
☐ A snowman who's out of this world

Grab your wallet and head back into to *Craft Show!* Can you find these silly things?

☐ A runaway gingerbread man
☐ A "door" prize
☐ A pickpocket plant
☐ Paul Bunyan's mom
☐ A pig in a blanket
☐ Pinocchio
☐ A *real fruit* cake
☐ A vampire

Dive back into the *Ocean* scene, and see if you can find these other funny things:

☐ A seahorse race
☐ An oyster bed
☐ A "cave" with an appetite
☐ The Good Ship Lollipop
☐ Three men in a tub
☐ A hotdog surfer
☐ A gold miner
☐ A school of fish

Hope you've got a sweet tooth! Go back to the *Candy Cane Factory* and look for these things:

☐ A sweet snowman
☐ A candy cane rapper
☐ A candy cane napper
☐ A guy with ants in his pants
☐ A worker carried away by his job
☐ A worker whose bubble hasn't burst